# THE MIND OF
# WALLO267 #2

# THE MIND OF WALLO267 #2

For more information:

@wallo267: [Instagram] [Twitter] [YouTube]
Bookwallo267@gmail.com // Wallo267.com
TEXT Wallo267: 267.214.4044

Cover design: @devkamera

Cover photo: @philmeyer__

Mind of Wallo267 & Mind of Wallo267 #2 transcribed by Amira Smith @amirasjawn

Layout design: dezinermama.com

ISBN: 978-1-64687-037-0

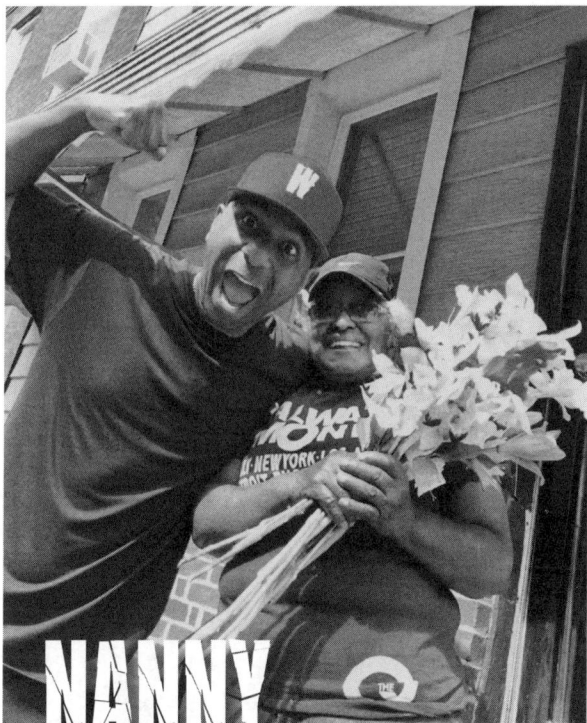

**NANNY,**

thank you for always pointing our family in the right direction. No matter what I was doing, you never gave up on me. During the darkest moments of my life you was right by my side. I love you YESTERDAY, TODAY, TOMORROW, FOREVER!

Your craziest grandson, **WALLY O**

# Contents

"I JUST FEEL LIKE WALLO'S TELLING US THE RIGHT STUFF. HE SPENT ALL THEM YEARS IN PRISON AND NOW HE'S OUT HERE PUTTING THE RIGHT MESSAGE OUT. HE'S AN OG THAT'S GON' TELL US TO STAY AWAY FROM THE THINGS THAT WILL TAKE US DOWN THE WRONG PATH. I WATCH HIS VIDEOS ALL THE TIME AND HE MOTIVATES ME. I COME FROM NEWARK, NJ AND IT'S EASY TO TAKE THE WRONG ROUTE AND GET IN THE WRONG SITUATION, BUT I COULD WATCH A VIDEO FROM WALLO—SOMEBODY WHO'S BEEN THERE—AND HEARING IT FROM WALLO KEEPS ME ON POINT."

—*Shakur Stevenson*
*(Olympian–silver medalist / Professional Boxer)*

# You've Just Been Conned

If you look like money, people gon' give you money. That's the reality of this. You might have a good product. You might have a good brand. You might have a good idea and you sitting here saying, *"Oh why nobody getting up on this?"* 'Cause you don't have the popularity. You don't look like money. You're not able to produce a lifestyle on social media that'll have people thinking you already won. See we come from a place where we only wanna support, encourage and nurture the person that we feel as though has won- the person we feel as though has got money. But if you see somebody coming up from the bottom, and you can support them, and you can help them, you like, *"Ehh- I'd rather buy it from over here 'cause they poppin.' They look like they're winning- they jumping off planes, you know, they leaning on foreign cars. They got jewelry on. They got all the designer clothes on."* That's the game! You've just been conned. YOU JUST BEEN CONNED! HA!

Introduced to the con game, you've just been convinced that this person's winning so that's the only reason you gon' support them. You just been conned. But the reality is we only support money. Money gets you money and the look is the hook, and that's the reality of life. So I need you to keep going. Forget the illusions and the con. Keep believing in yourself and it's gon' turn around for you. And it's just like that!

# You Gotta Walk Away

You're used to me running to you, but *today*, I'm gon' walk away. *You* gotta walk away. And when I talk about walk away, I'm talking 'bout some, "You know what? I'm holding onto something that's not holding onto me. I'm being a part of something that don't wanna be a part of me. I'm just right here in this world. I really don't feel like I'm accepted in this world. I don't really don't feel like I'm respected in this world."

This what you gotta do- it's simple as this: I'm walking away. I'm done. I can't do it no more. I'm not doing it no more. You know what, that not for me! I don't want that in my life no more. And you can even talk to them:

"I don't want that. That is not healthy for me. That is not encouraging to me- you know what? No, nah- i'm cool! I'm walking away. I'mma walk away- I'm just gon'

3

walk. You know what? I'mma walk away. No, no, no! I don't wanna deal with that no more- I'm growing! I know there's other places that's waiting for me and I can't go holding onto that. So I'mma walk! NO, no, no. Stop trying to debate- no you're not gonna convince me to stay. I don't even know I wasted more time dealing with you. I'm walking away. Thank you for educating me on what I don't need in my life. Thank you. I'm walking away."

# God's Gon' Test You, Then Bless You

I know you say you want this. *"I want this, I want that. I want that, I want this…"* See God gon' test you, then He gon' bless you, but you gotta deal with it. You gotta deal with the journey.

It's about that journey. That journey of, *"Oh do I really want this?!"* God gon' *continue* to test you. But if you're willing to go through it and you're willing to be dedicated- just like you're dedicated to him- He's gonna *bless you*. But it's not gon' be easy. It's gon' be hard. It's gon' be hard, I'm telling you, every day you just gotta keep going.

Keep going…
Keep going…

Keep going...
Keep going...
Keep going…

I'm telling you a lot of people are gon' doubt you. A lot of people gon' give up on you. You gon' give up on yourself sometimes. 'Cause I done been there. But you know what? You gotta PUSH THROUGH. PUSH THROUGH! God gon' test you. Then He gon' bless you, if you really want it! But you gotta push through. You gotta continuously push through.

# Don't Miss Your Train

The reality is you're gonna miss your train. The places that's gon' take you to the next level, the people that's gon' take you to the next level- you might miss them because you're involving yourself with people, places, and things that are not nurturing. It's not nurturing your dream. It's not going in the direction that you want to go to, so you're gonna be in the other direction somewhere else and you're gonna miss your train. You're gonna miss your opportunity. You're gonna miss your moment. Start being focused. Start locking in on where you're going. Start paying attention and giving energy to the direction that you wanna go. Stop going in the other direction. Stop being pulled in different ways. Stay focused. Wait your turn. Wait for the arrival of the train. Wait for the arrival of the opportunity that's gon' take you to another level in life, that's gon' take you to the places and stay connected to the people that you're trying to be a part of, and the places that you're trying to go. I'm telling you- listen: Don't miss your train. Cause you know what? I'm not missing mine. It's ready to stop and I'm ready to get on it. And it's just like that!

# The Truth is the Best Game

C'mon man. Let me explain something to you fellas. The best game is the truth. See a lot of times we think we're running game when we're lying to a woman, and we think we're a player when we lying. You not a player, you a liar. See, it was this one woman, I was talking to, she said, *"Wallo, be 100 with me. Keep it real."* I said aight, I'mma lay it on you. You want me to be 100 with you? I gave it to her. She gon' say, *"Ooh Wallo- you cold!"* I said hold up baby- I never knew that the truth has a temperature. You understand? You said you wanted me to be 100, I gave you 100- you only wanted 30. So my whole thing to all the fellas is listen, man, the best game is the truth. Always give a woman the truth so they can make the decision of if they want to travel through life under the conditions you presented to them. You dig what I'm saying? But you always give them the truth. Stop thinking that you a player because you're lying to 15 or 12, 3, 4, 5 different women. That's not a player, you a liar. The truth is the best game. And it's just like that.

# The Level Got Bigger, The Devil Got Bigger

Nah- this what you signed up for! Dig this- you gotta embrace what's going on. It's change that's happening and you know why? Your level got bigger and the devil got bigger. You sitting there and saying to yourself, *"Why is this happening, why is that happening?!"* If they're not slandering you, if they're not talking about you, if they're not changing on you, you're not winning! The ten got bigger, the sweat got thicker, baby! What's the matter with you?! This what you said. You said, *"I wanna win. I wanna go to the next level. I wanna change my bank account."* Listen, you lift your name, now come the change. That's a part of the game, baby. That's what it's about! You sitting there, *"Wah!"* Stop crying. SHUT UP! Shut up, be a boss.

Shut up and embrace the next level. Shut up and embrace the hate. Shut up and embrace the slander. Shut up and embrace all the change that comes with being a winner. You a winner, baby. Come on, now. Stop playing games. You wanna play. Listen, the level got bigger, the devil got bigger. He gon' come at you in all types of ways. He gon' do everything to stop you, to take you off track. So you won't go to your next level. But you're a winner and you gon' embrace all the changes that come so you go to your next level. And it's just like that.

# Convince Yourself

Let me tell you something man, if you think you can't have it, you won't. Because as soon as you get that thought in your mind that, *"I want this, but I'll just never be able to achieve that, I can't have that..."* All the ideas, all the ways, all the avenues, all the things you could do in order to get what you already convinced yourself that you can't have, because you're saying to yourself, *"Aww that's too big. Oh I ain't got a degree. Oh I ain't got this, I ain't got that,"* you done finessed yourself out of getting the things that you really want because you convinced yourself that you can't have these things.

Think about that. Why do we keep convincing ourselves that we can't do certain things, that we can't be certain people, that we can't go certain places. Why do we do that? C'mon, man. We gotta stop convincing ourselves. You'll finesse yourself right out of a situation like, *"Oh naw, naw, you ain't gon' be able to do that."* Nobody even had to do it outside of you. You got that in your mind, I don't understand why, cause you can do anything you want to do. You can go anywhere you want to go. You can be anything you wanna be. But you know what? You gotta put the work in, in order to do that. And you gotta be able to convince yourself that you can do it, just as you convinced yourself that you can't do it. And it's just like that.

# Everybody's Not Gonna Understand

I ran into one of my homies yesterday and he told me, *"Damn man, Wallo you on some other shit. And this, that and the third, man. You're different, man. You ain't like you was back in the day."* I said, "What I'm supposed to stay the same?" I said, "Let me tell you something, slick. You don't realize yesterday is over. That shit over with. We not young buls running around here with born to lose tattoos on our forehead no more and can just catch cases and do all this stupid shit. It's over, man."

A lot of people don't understand that you gotta let yesterday go in order to embrace tomorrow. And I'm like I'm out here doing some real legitimate stuff and I'm representing a bunch of people that I left in the penitentiary. I'm representing people that never even went to the penitentiary. I'm putting myself in the position to be the poster child that you can change after prison, and you worried about some back in the day shit?! Listen man- everybody can't go and everybody not gon' see it. And everybody not gon' embrace your growth, but you gotta understand: yesterday is over. That shit is over with. We can't be doing stuff we were doing when we were 15. And it's just like that!

# Dear Street Nigga

Dear Street Nigga,

I hope you make it through the night. I hope your mom don't cry when she gets that call that you're in the penitentiary or that you're laying on the ground expiring, as you're bleeding out. As the ambulance is getting closer you think they're getting farther because you're going to another place.

Dear Street Nigga,

I hope you don't be growing up in the penitentiary as your baby is growing up out here and another man is taking advantage of your baby and you can't protect your baby.

Dear Street Nigga,

Do you got some money to pay for your funeral? If you expire right now, did you create a trust for your baby? Do you got a deed to a house? What did you leave?

Dear Street Nigga,

The reality is, every neighborhood there's only a few street niggas that's getting money. The rest of y'all are just decorating the environment. Y'all are waiting to go to the penitentiary or killed, or just be a crash dummy to somebody else.

Dear Street Nigga,

I pray for you.

# The 'You' You Haven't Met Yet

NO, no no! Stop trying to escape that journey! That journey that you gotta go through, that journey of struggle! That moment in your life- you gots to go through that so you can be introduced to the you that you haven't met yet! And that you that you haven't met, that's the you that's gonna build you up! That's the you that builds character! That's the you that deals with adversity differently! So when you go through another journey in your life, you'll be able to travel through that journey smoothly. But you gotta go through the journey! This is not a cell phone. The journey is struggle. The journey that was written for you in your life is not a cell phone so you can't push reset. You gots to go through the journey! Stop looking for an exit! Stop looking for an escape! Go through it! So you can be introduced to that other you. That 'you' that can deal with situations that's tough! That's you! That's who you need to connect with! Stop playing games! You keep playing games! *"Oh I'm trying!"* No, no! Go through it!! Keep moving! Stay on that journey, you hear me? Stay on that journey and you gon' come out on that other side meeting the new you. You gon' be the new you. And it's just like that!!

# They Really Don't Hate You

To keep it all the way real with you, people don't really even be hating you, man. Because hate means to greatly dislike. You know what it be? People be hating the fact that you're able to execute on your idea. They be hating the fact that you're getting the attention. They be hating the fact that you're being able to make moves and that's what it be. They be like, *"Why they getting the attention and I'm not getting the attention?"* Or, *"Why they getting these things and I'm not getting these things?"* People have entitlement and they feel as though, *"I should be having these things. These things should be coming to me."* So it really don't be that they're hating you, they be like, *"Damn- why them and not me? Why them and not ME?!"* So sometimes

21

they'll just find themselves talking about you and a lot of times, believe it or not, they'll be advertising you. Letting other people know about you, because people will go check you out. Because I got some friends that's haters and they've introduced me to a lot of people that's informative out here in the game or were able to give me game. But I'm telling you- a lot of people, they really don't hate you. They just hate that they can't move like you and sometimes they try to outer-reflect how they feel about themselves on you, or try to throw it on you so nobody will look at them like that. But they really don't hate you. And it's just like that.

# Your Clique is Killing You

Clique, is killing everything that you want for yourself. Opportunities, relationships, doors openers. Your clique is disconnecting you from all that. See you don't know how to move by yourself so you gotta move around in a clique. But you don't know that when you're moving around in a clique, you inherit all their energy. You inherit all their problems. You inherit all their beefs. Everything that they got going on, you inherit that when you running around and you can't operate by yourself. And I'm not saying- you know me- teamwork makes the dream work, but sometimes we have cliques that we run around with. We have people that we run around with where it's no purpose, it's no plan. We just running around with them, just to be running around. If you party with somebody, that's who you party with. That don't mean you take them to every department of your life. That don't mean they gotta be everywhere with you. That don't mean you gotta be everywhere with them. But your clique is killing you. The cliques is the number one killer of opportunities and people getting to materialize their dream. Your clique is killing you. You need to stop letting your clique kill you. I'm telling you. You gotta separate yourself or you gon' be having to deal with everything bad they got going on. And it's just like that.

# Discover Your Why

You gotta discover your 'why'. Why should you be in a room with the life changers? Why should you be in a room with the check writers? Why should you be known for the best this, or why should people deal with you? What is your why? Did you discover that? Cause we always say, *"Oh I should be this. I should be in a position. I should be on this record label. I should have a deal. My salon is supposed to be the biggest thing... My business... my detailing shop... my car dealership... I'm the best real estate person... I-"* Why? Did you ever sit back and try to discover or connect with the 'why' that makes you better than everybody else? Why? What did you bring? Do you have any proof? Do you have a proof of concept? Why? Do you have any stats? Do you have any numbers to show? Why? It's all about why. It's not about everything else. It's about why. 'Cause that's what they're gonna ask you: *why you*? Umm-hmm. Why should I write this check? Mmm-hmm. Why should I financially back what you got going on? Discover your why. And it's just like that.

# When You Blow Up, They Show Up

The reality is, when you blow up they gon' show up. When you blow up, they gon' show up. Listen, that journey you're taking is gon' be a lonely journey. You gon' be by yourself. You know why? A lot of people think they're bigger than your journey. They think, *"Oh no, I'm too big to be struggling with them. I'm too big to be supporting them during their journey. I can't wait for them until they get stronger. No, I'm not gon' feed them with positivity. I'm not gon' feed them to make them keep moving. I'm not gon' give them that energy."* So when you blow up, they gon' show up, but you know what? They just gon' identify themself. They gon' identify themself that they a fraud and that they fake. And they only wanna be around for the win. They wanna come there for the celebration. *"Oh, let's pop the bottle!"* No! You can't be a part of the celebration. You know why? Because you ain't wanna be a part of the journey! You were too big. You thought you were too big, too this, too that, too popular for the journey. You ain't gon' be there. Don't show up when I blow up.

And it's just like that!

# Rule #1: Fuck What They Think!

**Rule #1**: Fuck what they think!

**Rule #1**: Fuck what they think.

When are you gonna start being more important than they? 'They' got so much power over you. 'They' got a hold of you. 'They' is the remote control of your life. 'They' the ones that dictate every move that you make. *"It gotta go this way- they gonna think this. I gotta wear this or they gonna think this. Oh, I gotta say this- they gonna think this. I gotta post this- they gonna think this."* When are you gonna start living for yourself, huh? Just imagine- when I first started doing my thing people was laughing. *"Oh, this nigga crazy. Oh, this nigga this, that, and the third."* If I'd have listened to them, my bank account wouldn't be on steroids right now. The opportunities that's coming to me wouldn't be. Listen- the things and the people that's in my email right now wouldn't be in my email and the opportunities wouldn't be there for me. *If* I'd have moved off 'they'. If I was worrying about 'they'. If I wasn't worrying about me. 'Me' supersedes 'they' any day! Any day! 'Me' supersedes 'they' any day. When you gon' start being in that position? When you gon' start thinking with that approach? When you gon' stop letting these people play you? Listen, man: **Rule #1**.

# If They Think You Crazy, You Cool

If they think you crazy, you cool. I don't care what you trying to do. If people are looking at you, you know, friends, outsiders, family, whatever, and if they're looking at you like you're crazy, you cool. You got plenty of time. Don't worry about it. You ain't gotta rush nothing. You ain't gotta worry about nobody competing with you. That's one of the best places to be. Where, *"Oh no they crazy, they tripping."* That's the best place. It was a place that I was at. That's why I had so much time. I didn't have to worry about me competing with nobody. I had better time to get my craft stronger. To get my whole approach better. Because when you on crazy status, nobody is paying you attention. So if they think you're crazy in what you're doing, you got plenty of time. Just chill. Just chill. Just go do your homework, do your research on whatever you're doing. The idea you got, whatever it is. I don't care what age you are. When people say that one word (crazy), or, *"Oh, they trippin' Oh, he crazy,"* you're winning. You're winning. You got an advantage. 'Cause ain't nobody- when I say nobody- they're not gonna pay what you have going on no attention for a while, but you cool. Just stay focused, stay dedicated and you gon' materialize your goals in time.

# Energy Disruptors

I'm warning everybody out there: be on the lookout for the energy disruptors. You know that person- that family, that friend, that mate. The energy disruptors. This is their whole spiel, *"Wahhh! Life is not happening for me! Shit just go wrong. I can't get a job. I wanna work out, but I don't wanna go to the gym. I want a job, but I don't wanna get off my ass and do something. I want this and I want that."* This is not dedicated to the babies, the elders or the mentally ill. This is dedicated to the bullshitters, the lazy and complainers.

*"Ahhh, it's happening for them, ahh ahhhh!"* Excuse me, do you live in America? *"Yeah, I live in America."* You don't live in a 3rd world country? *"No."* Well how are people from a 3rd world country coming over here making that shit happen? How are people just coming over here,

getting into America, and turning shit into millions of dollars, but you just sitting here and you bullshitting and complaining? Get away from those people in 2019. They will kill your battery. They will disrupt your energy. They're energy disruptors. Please get away from those people. I don't care if they're family, I don't care if they're mates. They're bullshitters, they're procrastinators, they're complainers. They're gonna point the finger at everybody, but themselves. And it's just like that!

# Stop Building a Stage for a Hater

You got to stop giving these haters attention. See, when you give a hater attention, you give them a stage. And most of these miserable muthafuckers never performed in their life. See, you make them a performing artist and they just keep performing. Once they drop they hate and you give them attention, they like, *"Ohh, my single poppin'! Oh they liking it!"* And they keep jumping on that muthfuckin' stage that you created for them. Stop giving these haters a stage. See, one thing about me, I never took no time-outs for the hate. When I was doing my thing and they was over here laughing and joking and hating, I ain't take no time-out to entertain the hate to say, "Oh who was hating?" I was like, yeah ok, and kept moving.

Yeah ok, and kept moving. I ain't never built no stage for no hater. Stop building a stage for haters, man. 'Cause once they get on that stage, they lose their mind. They gotta keep coming up with hate. When you kill them, like me- I ice them. I identify the hater and say ok. 'Cause one thing about a hater, they always double back. They always start loving you again. And when they come back to love you, you cut them off- in that way you ice them and you take the oxygen from them. Stop giving attention to the haters, and it's just like that!

# Salute a Player, Don't Shoot a Player

I ain't gon' shoot a player, I'mma' salute a player. Let me take that back for ya. I ain't gon' shoot a player, I'mma salute a player. And I go by players because we're all players in a game called life. At the end of the day, I was a guy coming up when I was knee-high to a butterfly, I'd see a cat doing his thing, he in the game, you know, '80s, '90s- whatever he was doing... I was the type of dude, I'mma salute you, "Goddamn baby!! Aww shit! I see you, man!!" *"Yeah, Wallo, you see me baybee! You see me!"* I'd be like, damn okay! Because when I see him doing what he was doing and he comes from the same ghetto I come from or he comes from a ghetto that looks like mine, different name, I said to myself that's just a notification that I can make it happen too. You know what I'm saying? This was before the cell phones. Cats were sending out notifications in the ghetto back in the day. And it was a notification that, yeah my mom struggled like your mom struggled and you can make it happen. But you always have a homeboy on the side saying, *"Man, fuck them niggas. We'll rob them niggas."* I'd be like, "Hol'- HOL' up baby! That ain't my type of hype, man. Listen, my breed don't entertain thoughts like that. Thinking like that would deactivate my thoroughness and I ain't wit that shit!" I was that cat. 'Cause I can always salute a player, I ain't gon' shoot a player. Salute a player. And it's just like that!

# The World In Your Pocket

The reality is, you got the world in your pocket. I remember when I first ran into a cell phone, I was in the cell. I had a cell phone for 14 months when I was in the penitentiary. They ran in my cell, took the cell phone from me- somebody told on me, whatever- they threw me in the hole. After that, I used to wake up in cold sweats dreaming about a cell phone. Because with a cell phone, you had a world in your pocket. You could do anything. The only thing that was more powerful than this before this came out was a pen or a pencil. 'Cause with a pen or a pencil you could do anything with also. But *this*? You could change the world. All the complaints you had, you have unlimited resources in your pocket. Anybody you want to connect with, you can connect with. Any world, any idea, anything you wanna do- it's right here on the cell phone. That's why I keep 3, 4 of them. 'Cause I'd panic without 'em. So what I'm telling you is, you have the world in your pocket. You have no excuses. Stop playing games. Get off your butt, go out there. *Take over the world.* Bring your ideas to life. Make it happen. And it's just like that!

# I Press Play Every Day

I blame me for not being where I want to be. I blame me for not being where I want to be. When I was in that dark place and when I wasn't where I wanted to be I had to blame me. That's why every day that I'm out here in this free world, I press play.

I press play every day. I don't care about nobody, what they're doing. I don't care about the weather. I don't care who don't like this, who don't like that. I press play every day. And that's how you gotta be in your mind. See you'll be sitting there, you be thinking so much. You keep thinking to where you'll overthink. You'll think about the idea, then you'll think yourself out of the idea. 'Cause you're thinking so much and you're taking everybody's opinions about what you should be doing. No. I press play every day. I put it together- ok, i'm pressing play on this.

41

I'mma have a list of things. I look at my list and say, oh I'm pressing play on this. I'm pressing play on number 57 today, but every day I press play! I say go. I don't care what you doing, how you doing, why you ain't doing it, if you're supporting it or not. I press play every day. That's how you gotta go. And I advise you: press play every day. Go after what you say you want, and I'm telling you, you gon' materialize it. I've been out of the penitentiary 23 months today. And I press play every day.

# Get Out There

The reality is you gotta keep going. No matter the situation you might be in, you gotta keep going. That's what I do, I just keep going. You better not give up. I'm not gon' let you give up on me. You not gon' give up on yourself. You not gon' give up on the people that's cheering for you, that's rooting for you. You can't give up. Why you keep playing? Stop. Go through it! Everybody goes through it. You're just in a rough moment right now. That's cool. We all go through these rough moments, but that doesn't mean you're just to give up. No, not on my watch. Get up. Get up right now. Get up. Get up off that couch. Get up out that bed. Get up out that slump. Get up out that bad- okay we understand you just went through a bad relationship break-up, you got job trouble- don't worry about that. You're still breathing- you got another

43

shot! What are you waiting for? Listen, get up right now. Get out there. Go out there and execute your plan. Go out there and materialize your dreams and do everything you wanna do. You're breathing so you're winning… and it's just like that!

# Dear Haters

Everybody's always talking about the haters. I gotta say something to you that's very important. First of all, y'all are some extraordinary individuals, but you know what? You gotta change lanes. You spend a lot of your time, you spend a lot of your energy hating on people. Think about it. Think about all the time and energy you spend focused on somebody else that's doing something that, more than likely, you want to be doing, but you're not doing it, 'cause you're focusing on the wrong thing. Anything on this planet that you want to do is possible. Especially if you have a phone- you could be doing anything. Whatever you wanna do. Business-wise, if you want to be an athlete or whatever. So that the time and energy that you're utilizing hating on people, talking bad about people, spreading rumors about people- whatever you're doing when you're on social media or just in life. Think about all the time you spend. Think about all the man-hours that you utilize to talk bad about somebody or hate on somebody. Think about if you switched that up. Turn that around and utilize that into bettering yourself, into educating yourself, into going after your dreams. Think about how great you are. Everybody's always beating up the haters. I'm not gon' beat you up 'cause I know nobody is ever on your side. So I'm on your side right now, letting you know that you're extraordinary. Make it happen.

# You About To Be Mad

You about to be mad. You about to be mad 'cause those ideas you had, you've been playing games with them. Those same ideas you got, you think no one of all of these billions of people on the planet, ain't got those same ideas? But you know what? You keep procrastinating. You keep BS'ing. And you scared to materialize your dreams. You just scared and you think you got time. You don't have time and you about to be mad, you hear me? You about to be extremely mad.

Then what's gon' happen is, somebody is gon' pop up with that idea that you been having, that you been laying on, that you been playing games with and you gon' be extremely mad. But you know what? You gotta blame yourself. You gotta look in the mirror. You gotta be mad at the person in the mirror because you had the plan all this time and you ain't execute it. You about to be mad. I'm telling you, and I'm warning you. Stop playing. Execute the plan that you've been holding on to inside of your mind and GO.

And it's just like that!

# I Give You Game So You Don't Take The Route I Went

Every day I used to wake up and say, "I'm going out there and rob somebody. I'm going out there and get some money." Every day. That was my whole game plan. It was like, I'm going out there to rob something, I'm going out there to get some paper the illegal way. Because I gotta get the things- I gotta get the clothes, I gotta get the money-in order to get the attention I need that was necessary in the ghetto. That was my whole thing. That was my everyday grind. So when I was in the penitentiary it was like, DAMN- all I was playing for was attention?! I was risking my life every day for attention? And the oldheads

49

told me when I was knee-high to a butterfly, *"Listen young blood, somebody gon' put you down and you're going to the penitentiary."* And I understood that. I understood that totally. But what happened was *this*: when I was in the penitentiary I realized the only thing I was out here doing this for was some attention. I just wanted attention from the girls. It wasn't even about no real money. Ya know, money was around. I had cats I could call to get some real live packages from, but I wasn't even with that. I just wanted small money, I just wanted something- that immediate attention. And that's what we were living for out here.

So when I'm giving you this game, I'm giving it to you from a cat that was out here married to the streets of Philadelphia. I know the game. So I'm giving you the game so you won't go the route I went. And it's just like THAT!

# Message To Frustrated Hustlers

To all you frustrated hustlers out there, what you gotta do is you gotta update your hustle. You gotta look at the world and say, damn I might have been hustling in the '80s, I might've been hustling in the '90s and that hustle and that approach that just hustling and getting your paper, that don't work no more. You gotta tap into this digital age. Don't be frustrated, don't be mad like, *"Aww these dudes ain't real hustlers!"* You're still talking about back in the day and the money you were getting back in the day and the moves you were making back in the day… *Playboy, this ain't back in the day.*

Take all of that frustration, utilize that energy that you use to be frustrated and talk about people and worry about, damn I ain't got this and I ain't got that- utilize that to do your research to tap into the new hustles that's taking place in the world today. These digital hustles. You dig what I'm saying? See a cat like me , I came home after doing all that time and I pimped my iPhone. You know what I'm saying? I've been macking on an iPhone. It wasn't like I had all this big team- no. Everything that you see that I do is off the iPhone. You dig what I'm saying? But I was a hustler from the '80s and the '90s and I just switched my game.

Message to all you frustrated hustlers: update your game.

# Validation Doesn't Lead To Elevation

People that don't matter. Validation don't lead to elevation. Stop worrying about that. You're looking for credit from the onlookers. Who are they?! They don't matter, but you'll be sitting there and be like, *"Oh they not showing no support"*- it ain't about support- you want attention from people that don't matter. What are you talking about? You're not really talking about they're gonna buy something, or they're gonna be this, or I'm doing this and they're gonna add value to this- NO! You're looking for attention from a bunch of people that don't matter. Stop seeking validation; it don't lead to elevation! C'mon, man! If they're with you, they're with you. If they ain't, they ain't. And the hard thing about it, most of the time it's gonna be family members that's gonna flake on you, that ain't gonna be there. But deal with it. C'mon, man! Everybody's always crying and whining! Shut up! Get out there and put the work in and keep going! All the people that's gonna support you, they're the people you don't know and they're the people all over this world. But *you* gotta go out there and connect with your consumers. And it's just like that!

# Popular Nobodies

You know, a lot of people chase popularity. That's why you got a lot of popular nobodies out here. They're not decorating the interiors of their bank accounts. You check their bank accounts and the shit look like an abandoned building. 'Cause they were chasing popularity they just wanted to be poppin'. If you're out here and you got dreams, go after your dreams, man. But don't chase: *"oh I just want to be popular, I just want people to know me"*, because a lot of times, that doesn't do anything for you. That don't pay your bills. You can't save no money up, you can't send your kids to college, you can't travel the world with that. And just look around. All these popular people on social media. Everybody that say they poppin', they poppin' this, they poppin' that... they ain't doing nothing. They're running in place, they ain't even get nowhere. Ain't nobody booking them. Ain't no checks. Ain't too much happening. You know why? They were chasing popularity- they didn't really have a real plan. They didn't really have a real dream. Their whole thing is, *"I just wanna be poppin'. I wanna be poppin'! I wanna be the wave."* The wave is a moment. The ocean lasts forever.

Don't be a popular nobody. Go after your dreams. And if you're going after your dreams and putting in that hard work, everything is gonna pay off. And it's just like that!

# Why You Keep Waiting?

Why you keep waiting? *"Oh, naw I'm waiting for this... I'm waiting to get money to do this... I'm—"* MOVE OUT!! Execute!! You keep waiting— you already know what you wanna do. But you keep waiting for that perfect moment. It's never gon' be perfect!! It's never gon' be perfect. When I came out, I ain't have nothing. I keep telling y'all this. I didn't have nothing. I had two phones, but you know what? I realized: you only eat what you kill so I had to kill everyday! That's why I was out here killing shit! You see me out here every day! You were like, damn is he gonna stop? No I wasn't gonna stop!! 'Cause if I was gon' stop I wasn't gon' eat! I wasn't gon' get closer to my dreams! So I had to keep going! I walked out of the penitentiary, I said I'm never going back!! But in order for me not to go back, I had to find a new way! And that's what I did, I found my new way. I didn't wait 'til I got money. I didn't wait 'til I had a crib. I didn't wait 'til I had this. I wasn't worried about that. I ain't have a TV in my room. But I went! That's what you gotta do. You gotta move right out 'cause it ain't never gon' be perfect. And you gon' keep waiting, and you gon' miss your turn. And it's just like that!!

# Hip & Cool Is Not Enough

You know, being hip and cool was more important than anything when I was coming up. That superseded everything. And in the 'hood I thought that was gon' take me all over the world. I thought that was gon' take me everywhere because that was important in my environment. At the same time, I'm being hip and cool- I understand that, I mastered that— but I ain't know how to read. So I was just a hip and cool illiterate dude. You na'mean? 'Cause being hip and cool was everything in our environment. That was the most important thing: being hip and cool and everything is gon' come your way. Because in the 'hood, I couldn't see far outside of what was going on in the 'hood. So I said, if I could operate under the hip and cool act, everything gon' come my way. Learning how to read wasn't important until one day I wanted to know how to read because it was something I wanted to know how to read, and *I ain't know how to read*. I was already in the juvenile system when I learned how to read.

So it's gotta be more than hip and cool. It's gotta be more than that. I learned that later on in life and it was a blessing that I was able to tap into that and realize the world is bigger than just being hip and cool in your environment. And it's just like that!

# The Grind Don't Get Tired

Let me tell you something, man: The grind don't get tired. The grind ain't got no vacations.

The grind don't get sick.

The grind don't got no off-days.

I had one vacation in my life: that was 20 years when I was in the penitentiary. Where I could sit back and do whatever. That was the only vacation I needed in my life. See, we keep talking about, "I wanna do this, I wanna go there." Listen, man. You gotta be dedicated to what you say you wanna get. Everything you're trying to do- you gotta be willing to do everything you've never done in your life in order to get to that destination, to that goal or whatever you want.

But all that chilling or, "I'mma party, but I ain't gon' get up in the morning," or, "I ain't got time to do this or do that…" That ain't gon' happen. The grind don't take no days off. And it's just like THAT!

# The Gun Changes You. You Become Someone You're Not!

Young bul, let me explain something to you. When you go and put that life changer, that gun, on your waist, when you go to play God— stop trying to be God— when you go to put that piece on your waist, your whole mind and mentality changes. Your energy changes. Now when a problem that's really not a problem comes to you, you're reacting different because you got that piece on you, because you're somebody else now. You're different than when you don't have that piece on you. So when you got that piece on you, you're saying to yourself, *"Oh, what?! What you say to me?!"* Now your whole demeanor changes. But you gotta understand, that when you got your piece on you, now you become a life changer.

You become a life changer and the life changer that you've become is a life changer that's gon' devastate. You're gon' devastate your community. You're gon' devastate your family. You're gon' devastate that person's family that you operate that piece on. You're gonna destroy the whole thing. See, a lot of dudes don't wanna tell you this shit because it ain't cool. You understand? See, I realized that cool was being me. Cool ain't trying to impress you to make you think that I'm cool 'cause you a young bul. I ain't got time for that shit. I ain't gotta be cool with you. You understand? I tell you this because I want you to save your own life and our community.

# Somebody By Your Side ≠ Somebody On Your Side

When I was young and I used to run the streets of Philadelphia, my oldhead Shavoy used to tell me, *"Just because somebody's by your side, don't mean they're on your side."*

When I was in the penitentiary I sat back and I used to think about what he said, and then E-40 and them came out with a song called, "Tell Me When To Go". And in that song he said something real important. He said, *"it's not just the cops, but the homies you gotta watch."* So I'm saying this to say to you that everybody is not gonna root for you. Everybody is not gonna cheer for you. And sadly, it's gonna be some people that's gonna be around you. It's gonna be some people that say they're for, or just might even say they're about you, but deep down inside they gon' have some resentment for you because they can't do what you can do. And they're also gon' feel a certain way because they're gon' be thinking that they're supposed to receive the things that you're receiving, but they're not willing to put the work in that you're putting in.

So you gotta understand: just because somebody's by your side, don't mean they're on your side. And when I was real young my oldhead Shavoy used to always tell me this, but I didn't understand until I was in the penitentiary and then E-40 and them slapped me in my face again. It's not just the cops, but the homies you gotta watch.

# Jump In The Mix

See, the reality is, you gotta get in the mix, because all human beings, we're all ingredients. But a lot of us don't come alive until we're in the mix. We get activated when we mix with other ingredients because a lot of us ain't strong by ourselves. You understand? It ain't nothing wrong with jumping in the mix. Getting deep up in the mix and saying, you know what? I gotta get with them and I gotta get with *them* because when I get with them I come alive. You get activated. Pay attention.

We're all ingredients. But a lot of us are just garnishes and we can't operate by ourselves. That's why we gotta get sprinkled on top of some food and then we come alive, because we decorate the scenery.

Jump in the mix and stop playing games. Stop thinking you're gonna make it happen by yourself. You're one ingredient by yourself, but you might need four or five ingredients to come alive and get activated.

Jump in the mix, and it's just like that!

# Friends You Haven't Met Yet

The reality is, strangers are friends you haven't met yet. You hear me? Strangers are friends you haven't met yet, but you gotta be willing to get out of that box. Get out of that small way of thinking and meet new people. Do human being things that human beings do:

"How you doing?"

"How you doing?"

"You got some nice shoes on."

"I like that hairstyle."

"I like your car."

That's what humans do. But you gotta get outside of that box. You see that box I'm talking about, you gotta get outside of that in order to grow. In order to glow. Strangers are friends you haven't met yet, you hear me? Stop being cool. Stop being too thorough. Stop being too hip.

Strangers are friends you haven't met yet. And it's just like that!

# I Can't Do It

No, this ain't got nothing to do with you. This ain't got nothing to do with you. This all me. I can't do it! You gotta get into that space in your life where you just can't do it. I got a homie, *"Damn, Wallo, where you at? Come get with me."* I know you still got the gun on you. I know you still operating outside of the law. I can't do it homie! This ain't got nothing to do with you. I love you, but I gotta love you from over here.

When you can't do it you gotta get to that place in your life where you just can say, "I can't do it." And you gotta say that to yourself. You ain't gotta say it to nobody else. "Oh, I wanna go to the club. Oh, I wanna do this. Oh, I wanna go to Miami. Oh, I wanna go to this." But I gotta pay my kid's tuition. I got these bills stacked up. I'm backed up on school loans. I CAN'T DO IT. That's where you gotta get to. See, that's the place that everybody's scared of. Everybody's scared of "I can't," but when you're saying I can't, you're saying you can't do something in order to improve yourself and you're putting yourself in a place that's gonna grow you. That's gonna glow you. I can't do it. That's what you gotta get to. Get to that place where you can say to yourself I can't do it because it's not gonna add value to the value that I already got for myself. I can't do it, and it's just like that!

# When You Gonna Start Being You?

Let me tell you something, lil bro. You out there, you being so cool, you being so tough. You trying to be so thorough, you trying to be so what everybody likes— you forgot to be you. When you gon' get some time to be you? When you gon' focus and say, "You know what? I'mma put this facade to the side and I'mma start being me?" Or when you just gon' say, "You know what? I ain't gon' have to focus on trying to get time to be me, I'm just gon' be me?" When is that gon' kick in? When is that moment gon' kick in where you say to yourself, you know what- I'mma stop trying to be cool for the dudes that really ain't cool. For the dudes that's frontin', just like you're frontin'. Guess what? You're a part of the frontin' conference of

America. Everybody frontin'. *"Oh, I'm cool. Lemme go over here with the cool dudes. Lemme go over here with the tough dudes. Lemme go over here with the thorough dudes."* All y'all dudes is frontin'. You know how I know? I was fucking frontin', man. But now, you know how good I feel every day when I wake up? 'Cause I can just wake up and be me? I can laugh, I can joke. I can just live my life. I'm out here living my life. But when you gon' start living your life? I'm Wallo267. Live your life, man. Stop frontin'. And it's just like that!

# Everybody Can't Go

Noo, no, no, no. We ain't gon' play no games. We ain't gon' play no games! Everybody can't go. Stop trying to make people the people that you are in order for them to go though the travel that you're going through. Everybody is not gon' be able to embrace your travel. Everybody is not gon' be able to fit in the car. You got two seats, but you're trying to take everybody with you. The reality is everybody's mind is not ready to go with you. They like where they're at. They like where they're at. You're trying to force them to, *"C'mon, c'mon, let's go!"* No, you can't force them to go 'cause if they wanted to go, you wouldn't have to force them- they'd be ready when you're ready. They'll have their bags packed when you got your bags packed. When you're ready to go wherever you're going, they'll be ready to receive where you're going and go where you're going, but they're NOT. Everybody can't go. You keep trying to force them. *"Oh, I want you to go. You're my family."* No, no, no, no- everybody's not a part of your dream. You gotta understand that. Sometimes you gotta come back and just visit. That's the reality of it.

Everybody can't go 'cause who gon' add value? Who's just gon' hang around? Who's gon' be an asset? Who's gonna be a liability? Who's gonna be a bill?

And it's just like that!

# What You Need Me To Do?

What you need me to do? How can I help you? What you need me to do?

See that's the reality. That's how you get in the game. When you see somebody making it happen and you're trying to be a part of that team, or you're trying to be a part of the winner's circle: what you need me to do? How can I help you? See that's the entry. That's the introduction. That's how you get inside the game. All that this, that, and the third- no. How can I add value to your value? How can I assist you? Do you need me to do anything? That's the game. Stop asking people for pictures and start asking them for game. We get around people and the first thing we ask them for is a picture. Hol' up- that person's in the field that you're trying to be in. Ask them for some game.

Deion Sanders told me when he first met Hank Aaron, he said the first thing I asked him, I ain't ask him for a picture, I asked him how was your mindset when you were chasing Babe Ruth's record? Think about that.

How can I help you? Start asking for game, stop asking for the picture. Do you need my assistance? And it's just like that!

# They're Gonna Laugh At You

See the reality is, they're gon' laugh at you. They're gon' talk about you. They're gon' say you crazy. And if they're not doing those things- if they're not laughing at you- you're doing something regular. See they're laughing at you 'cause you're different. You're laughing at them 'cause they're all the same.

You know me, people thought I was crazy. I come out of the penitentiary and they like, hol'- black man coming out of the penitentiary, people know him, he ain't selling dope, he ain't trying to be a rapper, he ain't trying to a tough guy, he ain't trying to do nothing that's gon' put him back in the jail. HOL'- he's a nut, like, what he on?! That's the mentality that people have. Because a lot of us need to be reprogrammed. We don't understand that. First we need to be deprogrammed so we can be reprogrammed. When we deprogram we get all of that BS approach to life out of us, period. Because it's been a mentality. That mentality is killing us.

But, they're gonna laugh at you. They're gonna talk about you. They're gonna do everything. But don't become discouraged. When you're doing something different and you're approaching life differently, people are not gonna understand that. People fear what they don't understand. Stay ten toes down in your belief, your approach to life, and your plan. And you're gonna materialize it. And it's just like that.

# The Grind Is The Key To Closed Doors

I learned early on that the grind was the key to open up the closed doors of life. That consistent grind, that dedication. Emory Jones once told me, "Wallo just stay the course." No matter what, never detour. Just stay the course and that's all you gotta do.

'Cause you'll be moving and your whole grind will be a key. Your grind will be a key. And it'll be a master key to a bunch of doors. You just gotta find them. And that grind that makes you keep going every time a door is closed, it'll keep you going and then you'll connect. That's everything. You gots to continue to grind. You gots to stay the course. A lot of us, we get fatigued. When it's a lot of doors, we get to the door and, *"wahh- that key don't work!"* No, no—

you got a master key to a bunch of doors- you just gotta connect with the doors that your key opens. And you connect with those doors when you stay consistent. When you keep grinding. When you never stop. You will be on top. I'm telling you, man. The grind is the master key to a bunch of doors. You keep grinding and you'll connect with those doors. And it's just like *THAT*!

# Focus On Your Dream, Not Your Nightmare

When you're living your dream, stop addressing or taking time out of your dream to address and give attention to your nightmare. You hear me?

When you're living in your dream and you're living in that moment, and you're doing your thing- stop worrying about your nightmares. That's over with. Focus on your dream. Nurture your dream. Make love to your dream. Travel with your dream. Hold on to your dream. Stop worrying about the nightmares because the nightmare's always gonna pop his head up, *"Look at me, look at me!"* Ignore it.

Yesterday is over! Let that yesterday go. Let them nightmares go. Focus on your dream and everything will be right. And it's just like *that*!

# You Gonna Get Tested

See the reality is, you gon' get tested. You know, we say we wanna do things. Man, I got tested every day. When I came home, I'm walking around, I got two phones, I'm shooting my videos, I'm making $200 a day. That was my hustle 'cause I used to sell 10 shirts a day. I had the 'It's Always Money in Philadelphia' shirts. That was my whole thing. Every day I sold ten. I went 37 or 38 days straight selling 10 shirts a day. Only reason I didn't sell them on the 38th day or 39th day, was because I ran out of shirts and I ain't notice it. But I was slamming them hard. At the time, it was so many people coming at me that I knew from the street game, knew from the penitentiary that was out here getting some street money. And they used to just come to me, *"Wallo you cool?"* They'd see me walking somewhere with my bookbag on. They'd see me in the rain shooting a video, *"Damn Wallo- what's up, man? You know I got such-and-such and such-and-such."*

We're talking about discipline, man. We're talking about staying down. We're talking about do you really believe in the dream that you have for yourself? I really believed in it. I could've made a call. I could've bought any drug that I wanted. I could have made any move that I wanted. But I believed in what I was doing. I believed in my message. I believed in who I became. And that's all it's about. You gotta believe in yourself.

# Stop Worrying About Everybody Else

See nobody ever told you, but I'mma tell you right now why winning ain't never been a friend of yours. See you be worrying about all the wrong shit. You be worried about everybody else- what they doing, how they doing it, how they making their money, how much money they're getting- you ain't got time to execute your plan. You ain't got time to be putting that positive energy out into the Universe and making shit happen because you be worrying about the wrong shit. You in everybody's business except yours. At the end of the day, you're tired, you go in the house, you go to sleep… you ain't execute your plan. You ain't do nothing you needed to do. You know why? 'Cause you were worrying about the wrong shit. See that's our problem. A lot of us be so envious and jealous and we get caught up. We be so caught up. And if somebody that looks like you whose mother went through the same struggle, came up, you can come up. But you don't see it that way. You take on this inferiority complex, you know, the jealousy and envy comes, it amplifies your insecurities and then you're done. Stop worrying about the wrong shit. Get out there and execute your plan. If anybody can make it happen that looks like you, you can make it happen.

# You Didn't Lose Them, They Lost You

Hold up- no, no, no. You ain't lose them, they lost you. They were removed out of your life because they weren't meant to be there. You all crying, *"Wahhh!"* You calling somebody, they got you blocked or whatever is going on- no! You didn't lose them, they lost you! Celebrate! Be thankful they're not in your life no more. Why are you trying to hold on to somebody in your life that don't wanna be in your life? That don't need to be in your life? That wasn't meant to be in your life? 'Cause the people that are meant to be in your life, they're right there. They're in your life permanent! You hear me?! They got a place in your life. They don't just have a place in your life, they have an apartment in your mind and your heart because they're meant to be there. Stop worrying about people that are not meant to be there. Stop worrying about the travelers. They were just meant to travel through your life. Like they said, people come into your life for a reason, a season, or a lifetime. The people that's in your life are meant to be there. They're there for a lifetime. They ain't seasonal relationships.

Stop worrying about who left your life and love who's in your life. And it's just like *that*!

# I Wanna Holla At Your Friend

I wanna holla at your friend- move to the side. No, you cool. Move to the side...

Yeah, friend, why every time your friend is trying to do something you always coming up with an idea of why they can't or you know somebody that tried to do what they're ready to do and it ain't work? You're always the bearer of bad news. Always bringing the information that something just can't work. Won't you just do me a favor and just shut up?! Shut up.

When you gonna start being a friend? When you gonna stop bringing all this negative energy? When you gonna stop bringing all this gossip? When you gonna start encouraging your friend? When you gonna start supporting your friend? When are you gonna start bringing things to the table that can enhance what your friend is trying to do, *"friend"*? Until then, *SHUT UP!* That's what you need to do: shut up. You don't wanna be supportive. Why is that? Is it a little envy or jealousy on the side because they're trying to do things and come up out of the situation that y'all are both currently in, that's gonna also benefit you? Hmmm. You ain't think about that. You just thinking about your selfish ways, but stop bringing information if it's not information that's beneficial. I understand being critical and giving somebody a different outlook, but your outlook is always dark. Why is it like that, huh? I need you to shut up, friend. *And it's just like that*!!

# Life Kicks Everybody Ass

This ass kicking you're taking by life right now? Listen, it's only momentarily. You're gonna be okay. You're gonna be cool. Don't worry about it. Listen, everybody gets their shot. Everybody that you see that's successful, everybody that you see that's winning, they've got their ass kicked by life. That's just the reality of life. That's a part of the journey through life. Life loves kicking people's asses to see if you're built. To see if you're ready to go to the next level. That's just a part of it. Don't look at it and cry and be defeated. No, you're gonna get back up. You're gonna get back up. It's gonna test you right now. That ass whooping that life put on you is just a test. You sitting there saying to yourself, *"Oh, the world's gonna end!"* No, it's not gonna end. No, not right now. It ain't gonna end- that's not what it's about. It's just about to put you through this to show you your strength. To show you that, you know what- when this happens again in life, I'mma be well prepared. I'mma have the experience to go through it in a more smooth way. I'mma be understanding of what's going on. That's all it's about. But listen, life kicks everybody ass. It kicked my ass for years on years on years and years and years. But once you go through and you get over it, you go to the next level. And it's just like that!

# Let It Go

See, a lot of times you just gotta let that go. Let it go. I done had people talk bad about me I never even knew. But you know what? I couldn't take it personally because they didn't know me personally. And let me tell you something— it feels so good when you just let it go. I done seen people, they done said this, and said that. It be cool. *"What's up, man. How you doing, man? How you doing, sis?"* I ain't got time for that. Because when you let it go you relieve all this energy that you'll be carrying around that's unnecessary. Let it go.

Let it go and you gon' glow. I'm telling you. When you're not carrying it— Because listen, a lot of times, we hold on and we embrace and we're receptive to other people's energy when we're taking on the things that they might say about us or whatever. We carry that with

95

us. Because you're sitting there and you're upset about something that somebody said about you. That ain't got nothing to do with you. That's their mind. They can say whatever they wanna say, but you'll carry it with you and you don't understand it'll mess your whole energy up. Let that go. Just let it go. People are entitled to say whatever they wanna say about you. But sometimes we gotta stop taking it so personal 'cause these people don't know us personally. Let it go. Please?!

# You Don't Really Want It

I've come to the conclusion that the reality is, that you don't really want it. Because you've got a thousand reasons why you *can't*, but you can't come up with one reason why you *can* make it happen.

I'm here in New York City, it's cold as hell out here, but you got a thousand people doing a thousand of the same hustles and everybody's making money. It's enough money for everybody. But you gon' sit here and say, *"Ohhh, I can't make nothing happen. Why me? My life is just nothing."* C'mon, stop bullshittin'. Stop bullshittin'. Get up, make it happen. Listen, man— let me tell you something, man. You got people that wake up every day that say, I'm tired of this shit. I'm tired of living this life. Look at all these vendors out here. They got the food out here selling, slamming sales all types of ways, hustling every type of way. But you keep talking about some, *"Oh, nothing's coming my way. Why not me? What did I do? God, could you help me??"* You keep praying to God— God already blessed you with all the resources, opportunities, already here on the land. It's already here. And He blessed you with air every day. He blessed you with the ability to get up every day, but you know what? You still got an excuse. Winning might just not be your thing. That's the reality of it. *And it's just like that.*

# Switch Your Focus

You focus on everybody except yourself.

You focus over there.

You focus over *there*.

You focus over there.

You focus *over there*.

But you never focus on yourself. You're measuring, *"Oh, damn they got this going on."* And then the hatred kicks in sometimes. The envy kicks in. *"Oh, they doing that?"* That's why you ain't winning. It ain't that you ain't got the energy. It ain't that you don't have the opportunities. It ain't that the information isn't out here. The information is out here. The opportunities are out here. The people that you need to connect to that will help you go to the next level, they're out here. But you can't take the focus off of everybody else and put it on yourself. You don't know how to just lock in on you. That's what it is. You're not focused on what you need to be focused on and who you need to be focused on. Your focus is all over the place. Everybody that you see getting these momentary wins or people that you feel as though are successful, or people that have all this material wealth? Your focus is on them. And sometimes with you being overly focused on them, that envy kicks in. That jealousy kicks in. That hatred kicks in. And that's why you can't win.

Stop being focused on everybody else and start being focused on yourself so you can get to the next levels of life. And it's just like *THAT*

# Pay Attention: Women Give Out Major Game

Let me talk to you about game. Since I was knee-high to a butterfly, I'm talking about a young cat shorter than a curb, women have given me the most game. When I was a young cat, there was this OG. He said listen man, you want some game? Listen to these women. So you know what? Since then, I've been listening to the women, catching the game up.

A lot of dudes probably can't take this information that I'm about to give them because a lot of dudes are approaching life on an egomaniac tip or a megalomaniac tip, where with them women are just, you know how it is, not on the levels or whatever. *But women?!* Women will lay some game on you, man. Pay attention. Because a woman, she wants to see you on a PJ (private jet). A regular dude, the average dude wants to see you on public transportation so they're only gonna give you a little/minimum game— they're not gonna give you so much. Because we're living in a competitive world when it comes to men. *But to women?* Listen, man. My show, *'Where's Wallo'*, my baby one day said, babe listen, you need to start a show. You're always everywhere. Then boom, boom, boom— I listened to her. I've done it. *'Where's Wallo'* is here and we're making it happen. And it's just like *that*!

# You Made Penitentiary Promises: Don't Act Up Now!

Don't act up now. Do not act up. You did all that crying in the phone room in the penitentiary. *"Yeah when I get home, I'mma do this. When I get home, it's all about my kids. It's all about you, baby, and my kids. It's all about this. Yeah if I can work in the kitchen."* You know how you be in the kitchen with your homie? *"If I can work in the kitchen for 19 cents, man, I can go out there and get a job."* But now you get out here and you fancy, huh?

You keep connecting with yesterday talking about the money you were getting yesterday. That's over with, man. That was 15, that was 18, that was 20 years ago. You're not getting that money. All that stuff— that's over with. You keep trying to utilize that as a resumé. That's over with! You can't use that as a resumé that you got money. That's over! You don't' get money no more, man. Go out there and get a gig. Ain't nothing wrong with getting a gig. You keep talking about you love your kids— go out there and do something. But don't come home with this attitude that you're entitled. Nobody cares about your rep. Everybody that was out here with you, they're gone. Put the work in that you told your family you were gonna put in when you were on that phone in the joint.

And it's just like *THAT*!

# You're Better Than What You're Doing

I'mma tell you something very important: You're better than what you're doing. I know people might look down on you. Got things to say about you. A drug might have you. It might have you being somebody that you're not. That's why I'm here to tell you: you're better than what you're doing. You might be in a place where like, you're just doing things— it might not be drugs, it might just be something that's outside of your character. Outside of everything that you've built for yourself. You disappointed your kids. You disappointed your family. You disappointed yourself. But I'mma tell you today! You're better than what you're doing! You hear me?! Don't let nobody look down on you. F THEM! I don't care who's looking down on you. I'm here to tell you today 'cause I know you needed this: you're better than what you're doing. Give yourself some time, but dig deep in yourself. Connect with that strength that you have. Turn back to who you were. It's never too late to be great. It's never too late to be what you would have been. You're better than what you're doing. I'm here to tell you. F everybody that's looking down on you. And it's just like *THAT*!!

# Start Believing & Investing In Yourself

You believe in everybody else, but you never believe in yourself. The athlete or the person on Instagram, you believe in them. You spend money, you invest in them. You buy their products, you buy this, that, and the third. But you know what? You never spend money to invest in yourself. You never just say, I'mma invest in myself and I'mma enhance my chances of winning and being successful in life in whatever department I choose to approach in life. Think about that. You believe in everybody— the athlete, *"oh, I believe they're gonna win! I believe this, I believe that..."* When are you gonna start believing in yourself? When are you gonna start investing in yourself? When you gonna start saying, you know what? This money I was gonna take and do this and that, I'm gonna take this money and I'm gon' invest in myself. I'mma get some more information. Or I'mma do this and I'mma do that. When you gon' start doing that, huh? Yeah, you don't wanna talk about that! *"Aw he trippin'."* No—I'm gonna force you to start believing in yourself, to start appreciating yourself, to start loving yourself. Start loving yourself. The same way we love all these people that you never met in your life and, most of the time, you're never going to meet during your journey through life. Start believing in yourself the way you believe in everybody else. Start investing in yourself, and it's just like *that!*

# The World Is Your Playground

See we gotta stop using a poverty measuring stick. As soon as we're coming from poverty we get a little bit of this, little bit of that, and we be like, *"OH, we made it! I made it!"* But the whole time you're looking at it like, *"Oh, I made it— I won!"* Nooo. You gotta start using a global measuring stick. The Earth is your turf.

Listen man, the world is a playground, so play. You gotta play out here. You gotta believe that you can have anything that anybody else in this world is getting. If you don't believe that you're in trouble. If you're just running around not thinking like that, you gon' be in trouble. If you're just looking at life like oh, I can't do this— I can only achieve this much. No! Stop using that poverty measuring stick and start using a global measuring stick for success. And you gotta understand that anything you want to do out here, you can do it.

But you gotta remember the world is a playground. So play!

# You Can't Clock Out On Your Dreams

Yeah baby! Talk to me! You can't clock out on your dreams! You keep talking about how you wanna make it happen. Stop taking sick days off from your dreams! You keep taking days, *"Oh, I did a 40-hour week. Oh, it's a 30-hour week."* NO— it's 24/7 when it comes to your dreams!! Why you keep taking sick days? Why you keep taking vacations? You keep clocking out. Like putting a timecard in a machine and punching the clock: *Click!* *"Oh, I'm happy to be off the clock."* How you happy to be off the clock and you talking about you wanna make it happen in life?! That's why you can't take it to the next levels of life. You're always saying, *"Oh, I'm trying to go here, I'm trying to go on this vacation. I'mma take off—*

*I don't feel like going in today."* HOW YOU NOT GON' GO IN ON YOUR DREAM?! Stop playing games with your dream. You cannot clock out on your dreams and win. You saying to yourself, *"Everybody else, they doing this and they doing that."* You know why? 'Cause they're always on the clock when it comes to their dreams! 24/7 when it comes to your dreams. Your dreams are worth 24/7! You can't clock out on your dreams. If you want to make it happen, never clock out on your dreams. And it's just like *THAT*!!!

# Everybody's Somebody

When I was younger, when I was a little kid, my grandmom Nanny, used to always tell me everybody's somebody. No matter where you're at in life. No matter what's in your bank account. No matter your living conditions. You're still somebody. And if you can hold onto that when you're going through whatever you're going through; just that belief and understanding that you're somebody. 'Cause everybody's somebody. It's not about being a star, or being an athlete; it's about you're somebody whether you're that or not. You just gotta hold on to that and know that you're special. Know that you're somebody. Know that things are gonna come your way. You just gotta stay down and believe in yourself all the way through it.

I remember when I was in that cell, I knew I was somebody. Even knowing that anytime these people could come in there and search my cell, strip search me or whatever— I still knew that I was somebody. I knew that I was a king with all that I was going through. I knew it. I just knew it. And that's how you gotta believe in yourself through adversity. Adversity will position you if you just hold on and believe.

Everybody is somebody.

# A Loss = a Time-Out To a Winner

A loss ain't nothing, but a time-out to a winner. It's that moment when you can regroup. That don't mean that it's over. That don't mean you're gon' lose the series. That don't mean the series is over. No!!

When I was in jail, guess what? I was a King, but I just was a captured King. When I had them shackles running from my wrists to my legs and they were shaking on that up-state bus, I knew I still was a king. Understand that. You gotta understand that. If you don't feel good when you're losing, you ain't gon' feel good when you're winning. You never really feel good if it's the winning that makes you feel good. It's the money that makes you feel good. It's the material that makes you feel good. But you don't truly feel good. You gotta feel good even when you're losing, 'cause you gotta understand something very important. A Queen is a Queen at the bottom. A King is a King at the bottom. It don't matter. It don't matter! I'll say it again: I was a captured King, but I still was a King. And remember this— what's real important: a loss is just a time-out to a winner. It's that moment that you regroup. And it's just like *THAT*!

# Ideas Are Cool, But

Stop playing games, man. You gotta stop playing games. People don't invest in who you used to be. And they don't invest in the idea of who you're trying to be. They invest in move makers and Earth shakers. At the end of the day, how can you make their money, make money while they sleep? That's what it's about.

It's about the bottom line. All that, *"I got an idea..."* and you just tell them how great you are in whatever you're doing. *"I'm a great business person... I'm a great this, I'm a great that..."* Nobody cares about none of that. How can you make their money make money while they sleep?! That's the reality of investors. Stop talking about who you were—nobody cares about who you were. Who you were is not relevant in the *culture now*. Think about that. And the idea that you have of who you want to be—no, what are you doing? Are you out here? Are you engaging? Are you in the mix? Are you move making and Earth shaking? If you ain't doing that, people don't wanna hear about it. People only invest in move makers and Earth shakers. And it's just like *THAT!*

# Thank You God

Thank you God for waking me up this morning and allowing me to be a part of your planet Earth. Thank you, God for giving me the air that's necessary for me to operate out here. Thank you God for putting all the tools necessary for me to win on this planet so I won't have any excuses. Thank you God for taking care of my family. Thank you God for getting me through the roughest time of my life. When I was incarcerated, I didn't know how I was going to do it, but for some reason, you pushed me all way through. You made sure I got up every morning. You made sure I had everything necessary, all the tools necessary for me to upgrade my way of thinking and to kill that old way of thinking that I had when I was operating outside of the law. Thank you God for putting *everything*, everything in front of my face when I'm looking for it. It just be right there. I be like damn, I gotta do this and it be like *BANG*— it pops up. Thank you God for forgiving me for my sins and all the things that I've done. Ya know, 'cause I never was perfect. I ain't gon' ever be perfect, but thank you for your forgiveness. Thank you for giving me this air that I'm breathing today. Thank you. And it's just like *THAT*!

# It's Never Too Late To Be Great

Let me share a story with y'all real quick. I'm standing right now at the corner of Broad and Allegheny (Broad Street and Allegheny Avenue in Philadelphia, Pennsylvania). See, right here on this corner, early '90s, circa like '92, '93, somewhere around there, right? I'm right here, doing a robbery. As I'm doing a robbery, my grandmom, she's coming across the corner, she's at the island in the middle of the street. I don't even see her. I don't think she knew it was me at first, but once she knew it was me she screamed my name. Once she screamed my name, I looked. I looked in her eyes and I've never seen this look in her eyes in my life.

A lot of times when you're out here in the street game, your mother or your grandmom, they know you're in the crime element— they know you're doing crime, but they never witness you or see you actually doing it. And for her to have to see me doing what I was doing, knowing that she brought me up better than that, it messed me up for most of my life. But I thank God. It messed me up for most of my life and I had to deal with that back and forth, but I'm glad that she's living to see me doing right.

It's never too late to be great. It's never too late to turn over and be somebody. That greatness. That great thing— that great somebody that's in you— to be that. I'm Wallo267 and it's just like *that*!

# Stay Away From Energy Vampires

If you've got dreams, you gotta go after them. You never know when life is gonna stop and it's gonna be all over for you. So the best thing that I can tell you is, number 1: stay away from those energy vampires that'll try to tell you what you can't do. The masters of what you can't do and why you can't.

Listen, you can do anything you wanna do. But at the end of the day, you gotta start doing *something*. Your ideas— you gotta take them off the paper. You gotta take them out of your mind and start trying to materialize them. And once you do that, then things will start going for you. Even if it's just the little thing of just doing some research. If you don't have the money at the time, just do some type of research. Start getting out there and networking with people. Get out there and try to find out how you can bring your idea to life with the little money you do have. But the one thing that's really important is you gotta stay away from those energy vampires.

The energy vampires, they'll stop your whole motion and they're always trying to tell you what you can't do. How is somebody gonna tell you something that you can't do and they've never done it themself. You can do anything. Anything is possible in life.

# Stop Limiting Your Options To Win!

When are you gonna stop limiting your options? When are you gonna stop closing your world? When are you gonna start realizing my approach to life limits my options because I got a negative attitude or can only see things a certain way? So by me seeing things a certain way, I'm closing my options. I'm not open to living. Think about that. There's a lot of things you can do out here, but you keep taking things off the table because of your mindset and your approach. The people, places, and things that you're dealing with might close your world. So now you can't see things in the big picture. You can't see the big picture. You can't look at the large picture and you know why? Your mind closed because it's certain things that

125

you say, *"I ain't with this… I ain't with this... I ain't with that..."* before you even learn a little about them. NO— you're limiting your options. Wake up. Stop limiting your options. Because when you limit your options you can't point at the world, you gotta point at yourself and blame you. And it's just like *that*!

# Dear Lil Homies, Stop The Goofy Shit

A few days ago, I come out of a corner store in Philadelphia, right? I run into this young bul that I know because me and his pop were in the joint together.

So he comes up to me, *"Damn, Wallo. What's up, oldhead?"*

I said, "Damn, what's up slick? What's going on?" He's out here moving and grooving— doing his thing how he do it— that's his business,— but dig this:

He says to me, *"Man, I gotta holla at you for a minute."*

I said, "What's up?"

He said, *"Man, they just gave my homie life plus 20 to 40. Damn man, how do that run? Like, how do that work?"*

I said, "Well in Pennsylvania that means he gotta do the life first, he gotta die, he gotta come back and he gotta do the 20 to 40."

He talking about, *"Whatchu— what? What you talking about? What that mean?"*

I said, "He gotta do the life bid first— the life sentence— 'cause in Pennsylvania, life means life. Life means you don't get out until you die. You nahmean? You die and that's when you get released— when you stop breathing. Once that's through they're gonna take him to the graveyard, have his funeral, then he gotta come back to jail and do the other 20 to 40 years."

He said, *"Man, what?!"*

I said, "That's what it means."

He said, *"Aww man, I ain't on that— I..."*

I said, "Well stop the goofy shit, then. Stop running around here with this goofy crime shit. That's what you need to do."

# I Will Never Stop!

*I don't care what nobody says!* It's gonna be times in life— *it's gon' be them times! I've witnessed those times!!* I was this close— you've got the graveyard and you've got the penitentiary— *I was at the lowest stages of life, but you know what?! I kept going and I said when I get back up, I will not stop!!* I will not!! Listen, I'm not gon' stop 'til my casket drops!! And when my casket drops, let me tell you something— the energy that I'mma leave on this planet gon' be so powerful that it's gon' keep moving. It's gon' keep growing. It's gon' keep showing. It's gon' keep glowing.

*Nothing can stop you!!* Nothing can stop you, you hear me?! Can't nobody stop you!! Nobody can stop you!!! *I've been there!! I was at the bottom of life!! I was at the darkest place that you can be while you're breathing!!* But you know what?! I said I'mma get back and I'm gonna be better than I was yesterday and when I get back, *I'M NOT GONNA STOP!! I WILL NEVER STOP!!!* YOU BETTER NEVER STOP!! I don't care what nobody says: you better not never stop. **YOU CAN MAKE IT HAPPEN!! YOU CAN MAKE IT!!**

# My Dash

The reality is we ain't gon' be here long. When you come in the graveyard— listen, when I stop breathing, and you come in the graveyard, as you're approaching you're just gonna hear music playing. The energy gon' be so powerful on my tombstone because I understand that dash. That dash— that year you were born and the year you died, that dash in between— what do you want your dash to be?

You know what my dash gon' be? My dash gon' be amazing. It's gon' still be moving because the things that I'mma do in life, they gon' live beyond life. I'm talking about it's gon' be out of this world. You know why? Because every day, I'm out here living. I live my life every day. I live like it's my last day on Earth every day. I do what I wanna do. **That's the power.**

You gotta get the power of doing what you wanna do. What goes on down my timeline, the stuff I see on the timeline, the stuff I see on Instagram— that don't dictate my life. I don't care what they're wearing on Instagram. I don't care where they're going on Instagram. I don't care what they got on Instagram. **I live my life. I own me.** Guess what? I'm the CEO of me. What do you want your dash to be? Is it gon' be flat? Is it gon' be moving? Mine is gon' be moving and grooving, baby. **And it's just like that!**

# Your Attitude Is Killing You

It's your attitude. Your attitude is killing you. Your attitude keeps making those doors close. You know why? Every time you hear things that you're just not receptive to, things that don't sound good or soothing to your ear, or your ego— you just switch up. It's on your face. It's in your whole body language. Think about that. Attitude is everything. I don't care how much talent you have. I don't care how many moves you feel you can make. When it's time to go to the next level, the life changers, the people that can open the doors, that can make it happen for you? They're gonna go, *"Hol'-- hold up..."* You're gonna rub them the wrong way. It's your attitude. You keep wondering why this ain't happening and why it's happening for them—

first of all, stop watching other people. Stop counting and watching other people. You're counting people— No, no— that's not what your job is. You're not the census. So stop worrying about other people and counting other people. What you need to worry about is you need to look in the mirror. You need to check your attitude and once your attitude is right, and then your execution is right, everything is gon' happen for you. But until your attitude changes and your approach to life changes, ain't nothing gonna happen for you. And it's just like *that*!

# Be Thankful For All Blessings

You gotta stop complaining about them blessings. You sitting there and you're complaining: *"Oh this ain't come, that ain't come!"* Hold up, hold up. Just because you can't identify a blessing because it ain't a blessing that you requested, you complaining?

Think about this. I had this cellmate. I had 10 years in with 10 years to go. He's my cellie. Every day he's crying. *"Oh, I can't wait 'til I make parole. I wanna make parole."* He made parole. So when it was time for him to go home they told him, *"Listen, you can't go to this halfway house, you gotta go to* this *halfway house."* Don't you know he had the nerve to come back in the cell and complain to *me* and I still had 10 years to go?! I said, "hold up man— you just got blessed. You're going home. I gotta sit here. Why you keep complaining?" And you know what? He went home… 3 months later he was back. What I'm saying is, we gotta be thankful for the blessings when they come.

Just because it ain't the blessing we requested, we can't be all crying and whining. Shut up! Start being thankful. Just because you can't identify a blessing because it ain't the one you requested doesn't mean you can't accept it and be receptive to the blessing. And it's just like *THAT*!

# Slow Pace Is Better Than No Pace

You gotta understand something that's very important. Slow pace is better than no pace. Let me say this again: slow pace is better than no pace. You're looking at other people's blessings and you're trying to expedite your blessings. And you're asking God or you're asking people, *"Why they doing this? Why they doing that?"* Instead of waiting your turn. Slow pace is better than no pace. You're moving. You're gonna get to your destination that you wanna be at in life, but you ain't gon' get there worrying about everybody else.

You need to take the time and the energy that you're utilizing and worrying about somebody else— you're just tapped into and zooming in on their blessings, and start putting that energy into you. Into materializing your dream. Listen, God gives you opportunities. But God ain't just gon' hand it to you like, *"Here you go."* No, no. You gotta put that work in. He gives you the knowledge and the know-how, the legs, the feet, the mouth to go out there and make it happen.

But listen, slow pace is better than no pace. Stop rushing the process. Stop trying to expedite your blessings. *It's not gonna happen like that.* Sit back, wait your turn. Get out there. Execute the plan. And make it happen. Stop complaining. Slow pace is better than no pace. And it's just like that!

# Opinion = Hate Where I'm From

First and foremost, it's called an opinion. And you can have that. But for some reason, in the hood, if your opinion doesn't align with somebody else's opinion, or somebody else's views— *"I like brown."* "Oh, I don't like brown, my favorite color is black or my favorite color is green." *"Oh, you's a HATER!"* And don't let a person be popular. If they're popular, and you speak about them and you ain't in agreement with what their approach to life is, or what they have going on, you're a hater. Hmmm... that's deep. I understand haters are your marketing team, let them work, but we gotta really think about the word hater. And we gotta think about how we're approaching this whole thing and how we be tripping out.

At the end of the day, people are allowed to have their opinions. Common once said, "If I don't like it, I don't like it. That don't mean that I'm hating." For example, everybody doesn't drink cranberry juice. Just because you drink cranberry , and you like to drink cranberry juice with your cheese eggs— I might don't like cheese in my eggs— oh, I'm a hater now? Naw it ain't like that.

We gotta change our mindsets. And we gotta open our minds up to realize that everybody has an opinion. And it's just like that.

# Can You Handle?

We say, *"I want this. I want love. I want that. I want this. I want this type of partner. I want a partner that's winning. I want a partner that's on the next level. I want a partner that's doing this, that, and the third. I want a husband. I want a wife that's doing* this." Let me ask you a question. What's more important than all this: Can you handle the lifestyle of the partner that you're seeking?

Can you handle their yesterdays? Can you handle their shortcomings? Can you handle the hardships they go through and will continue to go through? Can you handle that? No. Oh, you just want the celebration part of the whole relationship. You just wanna be happy every day. Could you handle their upbringing and everything that they went through? The trauma, the abuse? Can you handle that? If you can't handle that, stop saying you're

141

looking for somebody. Stop saying you want a partner. You gotta take on all that. Can you handle that their child might be going through something because their father is not there? Can you handle that?

Are you ready to accept and deal with the lifestyle and the struggle that comes along with loving another human being? Ask yourself that.